O9-BTJ-882

The Colony of Massachusetts

Susan Whitehurst

The Rosen Publishing Group's
PowerKids Press™
New York

Published in 2000 by The Rosen Publishing Group, Inc.
29 East 21st Street, New York, NY 10010

Photo Credits: pp. 1, 6, 8, 12, 15, 19, 20, 22 © Super Stock; p. 4 © Victoria & Albert Museum, London/Art Resource; p. 7 © Private Collection/ Super Stock; p. 11 © Super Stock Inc. Collection, Jacksonville/Super Stock; p. 16 © Corbis-Bettmann;

First Edition

Book Design: Andrea Levy

Whitehurst, Susan.
   Massachusetts / by Susan Whitehurst.
      p.   cm. — (The Library of the thirteen colonies and the lost colony)
   Includes index.
   Summary: An introduction to the early days of Massachusetts colony, from the difficulties faced by the Pilgrims to the role of Massachusetts in the American Revolution.
   ISBN 0-8239-5475-7
   1. Massachusetts—History—New Plymouth, 1620–1691—Juvenile literature. 2. Massachusetts—History—Colonial period, ca. 1600–1775. 2. Pilgrims (New Plymouth Colony)—Juvenile literature. [1. Massachusetts—History—Colonial period, ca. 1600–1775. 2. Pilgrims (New Plymouth Colony)] I. Title. II. Series.
F67 .W495 1999
974.4'02—dc21
                              98-32369
                                CIP
                                AC

Manufactured in the United States of America

Contents

Leaving England

In the 1600s, King James I of England said everyone had to belong to his religion, known as the Church of England. If they didn't, they could lose their homes and jobs. They might be sent to prison, or even hanged. People called **Puritans** were not happy with the English church. They believed that it allowed people too much **luxury**. The Puritans thought life and religion should be pure and simple. In 1620, a group of these Puritans, called **Pilgrims**, left England for America. They hoped they would be free to practice their own religion there. The Pilgrims planned to settle in the **colony** of Virginia, but the Pilgrims' ship went off course and they ended up settling a new colony: Massachusetts.

King James I was in charge of England's church and its government in the 1600s.

Hard Times in Plymouth

In September of 1620, 70 adults, 32 children, some chickens, and two dogs sailed for Virginia on a ship called the Mayflower. Winds blew the ship off course, and the Pilgrims landed in a place they called Plymouth, after the town they had come from in England. Before they got  off the boat, the Pilgrims wrote the Mayflower Compact. In it they said they would all work together, vote to make decisions, and do what the **majority** wanted. The Pilgrims reached Plymouth when it was too late to plant food. Half of the Pilgrims died that first winter. By spring, there were only 50 colonists left, and half of those were children.

The Pilgrims were aboard their ship, the Mayflower, (shown above) for a little over two months before landing on New England's rocky coast. ▶

The First Thanksgiving

In 1621, the Pilgrims were struggling to survive. **Algonquian** Indians had lived in the area for hundreds of years. They knew all about the land and how to grow food. Two Indian men, named Samoset and Squanto, were curious about the colony and came to get a closer look. At first the colonists were afraid, but they soon made friends with the Indians. Squanto played a big part in helping the settlers hunt, fish, and farm. In the fall of 1621, the Pilgrims were thankful to be alive and thankful to the Indians for their help. They decided to have a feast to give thanks. Ninety **braves** came to the first Thanksgiving.

When Christopher Columbus first reached the New World, he thought he had landed in Asia, then called the Indies. He called the local people "Indians."

For three days, everyone sang, danced, and played games. They ate deer, corn bread, vegetables, turkey, lobster, and eel.

9

Massachusetts Bay

Back in England, Puritans were still **persecuted**. In 1629, a group of Puritans organized a company called the Massachusetts Bay Company. They got a **charter** from the King to settle in America. Between 1629 and 1640, more than 20,000 settlers came to the Massachusetts Bay colony. The Puritans in Massachusetts had very strong religious beliefs. They felt that the church in England was not pure enough in its beliefs and practices. They hoped to make it better. John Winthrop, the **governor** of Massachusetts, said that he hoped to have a society that was so good and moral that people back in England would want to imitate it.

The Puritans believed in hard work. This belief that hard work is the way to success is still important in the United States. Since the hardworking Puritans were Protestant, this belief is sometimes called the "Protestant work ethic."

Winter in Colonial Massachusetts was a particularly hard time for the Puritans. They had to work together to survive. ▶

Conflict with the Indians

As more Englishmen came to Massachusetts, they claimed more land. Colonists started moving into areas where Native Americans had lived for hundreds of years. In 1636, colonists said that Pequot Indians had killed two traders. The colonists attacked a Pequot town, killed many of the people there, and claimed their land. In 1675, a Wampanoag Indian leader called Metacom stood up to colonists who were moving into Indian land. Fighting between the Indians and the settlers lasted through 1676. Metacom was captured and killed during the war. One thousand other Indians were sold as slaves.

Metacom was called King Philip by the English. The war with the Wampanoag Indians is called King Philip's War.

Squanto and the early Massachusetts colonists worked together, but as colonists took more and more land, Indians who had lived there first started to get angry.

13

The Dominion of New England

In 1686, King James II of England said that the colonies could not have their own governments. He joined all the colonies from Massachusetts to New Jersey together into one colony called the Dominion of New England. The head of the Dominion was Sir Edmund Andros, a leader chosen by the King. Andros would not allow Dominion citizens to elect members of the government. New England colonists were angry because they were not allowed to pick their leaders, or to vote on **taxes**. In 1688, King James II was overthrown. The colonists **revolted** and sent Andros back to England, but Massachusetts still did not get to rule itself. The new King and Queen, William and Mary, made Massachusetts a **Royal colony** in 1691.

Colonists had come to Massachusetts for religious freedom. Now they wanted political freedom, too. ▶

14

The Salem Witch Trials

The Puritans had come to America to escape religious **intolerance** in England, but the Puritans themselves could be intolerant. They were **suspicious** of any practices or beliefs that were different from their own. In the 1600s, some Puritans

During the Salem witch trials, nineteen people were hanged, one was pressed to death, and two dogs were killed. People thought that witchcraft was making them do bad things. Later, these people realized that they had made a mistake.

started to fear that people were practicing **witchcraft**. Witchcraft could take many forms, but the basic idea was that witches had **supernatural** powers, which they could use to hurt other people. This fear got out of hand in Salem, Massachusetts, between 1692 and 1693. During the Salem witch **trials**, twenty people were put to death.

The witch trials in Salem, Massachusetts, were one of the worst examples of fear and intolerance getting out of control in Colonial America.

Tea and Taxes

Although the colonists were far from their country, they were still English. To make money to help pay for the French and Indian War, which England had just fought with France from 1754 to 1763, the King decided to tax the colonists in America. The taxes made sugar, paper, newspapers, and tea cost more money. The colonists didn't think it was fair that they couldn't vote in the English government, but still had to pay English taxes. Not being able to vote about what you're going to be taxed for is called "taxation without representation." Some colonists decided that they wouldn't buy any of the products the King had taxed. Fifty colonists were so mad about the tea tax that they threw three shiploads of tea into the Boston Harbor. This act was nicknamed the Boston Tea Party.

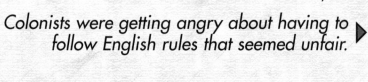

Colonists were getting angry about having to follow English rules that seemed unfair. ▶

The Fight for Independence

The King sent soldiers, called Redcoats to Massachusetts to punish the colonists for not obeying his laws. Colonial farmers and shopkeepers were trained as soldiers so that they would be ready when the British attacked. Paul Revere became famous for his midnight ride, which warned colonists of the Redcoats' arrival. The first shot of the American Revolutionary War was fired in Massachusetts in 1775. After the war, the colonists were free from England. They made their own rules and called themselves the United States of America. Massachusetts signed the **Constitution** and became a state in 1788.

Paul Revere was so proud of his part in the War that he wore his Revolutionary War uniform every day for the rest of his life.

◀ *On his horseback ride, Paul Revere yelled, "The British are coming!"*

Massachusetts Today

If you visit Massachusetts today, you will see many towns built around village greens, just like the Puritans used to build their towns. A Pilgrim village has been rebuilt in Plymouth, Massachusetts. The homes and shops there show how the Pilgrims used to live in Colonial times. Plymouth Rock, the spot where the Pilgrims first landed, still sits on the beach. It is marked by a **monument** (shown above). Nearby is the Mayflower II, a ship built to look like the one that carried the Pilgrims to Massachusetts almost 400 years ago. You can climb aboard and imagine how the Pilgrims felt when they started a new life and helped build a new nation.

1620	1764		1776
The Pilgrims sail from England on the Mayflower in September.	England begins to tax the colonists.	The Revolutionary War begins in Lexington and Concord, Massachusetts.	Massachusetts signs the Declaration of Independence.
The Puritans sail from England to Massachusetts.			Massachusetts signs the Constitution and becomes a state.
1630		1775	1788

Glossary

Algonquian (al-GAHN-kwee-in) Indian tribes living for many years in New England.

brave (BRAV) Indian men trained to fight.

charter (CHAR-tur) An official paper giving someone permission to do something.

colony (KAH-luh-nee) An area in a new country where a large number of people move, who are still ruled by the leaders and laws of their old country.

Constitution (kon-stuh-TOO-shun) A paper that explains the rules of the American government.

governor (GUH-vuh-nur) A political leader in a state or colony.

intolerance (in-TAL-ur-ints) Close-minded and not willing to accept other people's ideas.

luxury (LUK-shu-ree) Something that is nice or expensive, but is not really needed.

majority (muh-JOR-ih-tee) The most or the greatest number of something.

monument (MAHN-yoo-ment) Something built to honor a person or event.

persecuted (pur-sih-KYOO-tid) When people are attacked or treated badly.

Pilgrims (PIL-grumz) The first group of Puritans to leave England and come to America.

Puritans (PYUR-ih-tinz) A group of Christians who wanted religion in England to be simpler.

revolt (ri-VOLT) To fight or rebel.

Royal colony (ROY-ul KAH-luh-nee) A colony whose rules were made by England.

suspicious (suh-SPIH-shus) To believe that someone is bad or guilty without proof.

supernatural (soo-per-NAH-tur-ul) Unnatural power or ability.

tax (TAKS) Money that people give the government to help pay for public services.

trial (TRYL) A contest held in court to prove or disprove something.

witchcraft (WICH-kraft) Using sorcery, magic, or unnatural powers.

Index

Web Sites:

You can learn more about Colonial Massachusetts on the Web:
http://www.geocities.com/Athens/Oracle/5650/mass.htm